ON THE NEXT PAGE, WE WILL BEGIN TO FIND OUT,

WHAT A BRAIN IS ALL ABOUT, WITHOUT A DOUBT!

IN YOUR HEAD, THERE IS SOMETHING NEAT,

A BRAIN, IT MAKES EVERYTHING COMPLETE

LIKE A BOSS, IT TELLS WHAT TO DO,

WITH NEURONS, IT IS A CLEVER CREW!

WHEN IT'S TIME FOR SLEEP AND DREAMS TO START,

YOUR BRAIN PLAYS ITS SLEEPYTIME PART.

IT TELLS YOUR BODY, "REST YOUR HEAD,"

AS YOU SNUGGLE UP IN YOUR COZY BED.

AND WHEN THE SUN BEGINS TO RISE,

YOUR BRAIN WAKES UP, OH, WHAT A SURPRISE!

IT SAYS, "GOOD MORNING, TIME TO PLAY,"

AND YOU ARE READY FOR A BRAND NEW DAY.

YOUR BRAIN IS THE REASON FOR LAUGHTER'S SOUND,

IT SPREADS JOY AND MAKES YOUR HEART REBOUND.

WHEN GIGGLES AND SMILES FILL THE AIR,

IT IS YOUR BRAIN THAT TAKES YOU THERE.

BUT, MY DEAR, REMEMBER THIS REFRAIN,

YOUR BRAIN ALSO KNOWS ABOUT SOME PAIN.

IT HELPS YOU LEARN AND HEAL, IT IS TRUE,

WHEN THINGS IN LIFE MAKE YOU FEEL BLUE.

WHEN YOU RUN, JUMP, OR EVEN SIT WITH GLEE,

YOUR BRAIN'S THE CAPTAIN, YOU WILL SOON SEE.

IN EVERY MOVEMENT, BIG OR SMALL,

YOUR BRAIN IS IN CHARGE, THE RULER OF ALL.

AND DURING MOMENTS OF PEACEFUL REST,

YOUR BRAIN KEEPS WORKING, IT'S TRULY THE BEST.

IT ENSURES YOUR HEART BEATS WITH RHYTHMIC GRACE,

AND YOUR LUNGS BREATHE AT A STEADY PACE.

DEEP INSIDE YOUR BRAIN, A WONDROUS SIGHT,

NEURONS WORK, DAY AND NIGHT.

THEY'RE LIKE TINY MESSENGERS, OH SO SMALL,

HELPING YOUR BRAIN, THEY DO IT ALL!

IMAGINE A NEURON, A VERY THIN STRING,

IN YOUR BRAIN, IT HELPS THOUGHTS DO THEIR THING.

IN THE THINKING WORLD, IT PLAYS A ROLE VERY SMART,

STITCHING THOUGHTS TOGETHER LIKE A PIECE OF ART.

NEURONS PASS MESSAGES TO AND FROM,

LIKE SUPERHEROES ON THE GO.

THEY HELP YOU THINK, THEY HELP YOU PLAY,

IN THE MOST AMAZING, FANTASTIC WAY.

LIKE FRIENDS WHO TALK IN A SPECIAL WAY,

THEY SEND TINY GIFTS TO EACH OTHER EVERY DAY.

THESE LITTLE GIFTS HELP THEM SHARE WHAT THEY KNOW

THAT'S HOW OUR BRAINS LEARN AND HELP US GROW!

TO KEEP NEURONS HAPPY, STRONG, AND FINE,

EAT HEALTHY FOODS, LIKE FRUITS AND BRINE.

AND DON'T FORGET TO SLEEP REAL TIGHT,

SO NEURONS WORK WELL DAY AND NIGHT!

Made in the USA
Coppell, TX
03 April 2024

30882869R00017